PIANO/VOCAL SELECTIONS

LINCOLN CENTER THEATER
. UNDER THE DIRECTION OF

André Bishop and Bernard Gersten

PRESENTS

THE LIGHT IN THE PIAZZA

BOOK	MUSIC AND LYRICS
Craig Lucas	Adam Guettel

BASED ON THE NOVEL BY Elizabeth Spencer

WITH (IN ALPHABETICAL ORDER)

Glenn Seven Allen   Michael Berresse   Sarah Uriarte Berry   David Bonanno
David Burnham   Victoria Clark   Patti Cohenour   Beau Gravitte   Laura Griffith
Mark Harelik   Prudence Wright Holmes   Jennifer Hughes   Felicity LaFortune
Catherine LaValle   Michel Moinot   Matthew Morrison   Kelli O'Hara   Joseph Siravo

SETS	COSTUMES	LIGHTING	SOUND
Michael Yeargan	Catherine Zuber	Christopher Akerlind	ACME Sound Partners

ORCHESTRATIONS	ADDITIONAL ORCHESTRATIONS
Ted Sperling and Adam Guettel	Bruce Coughlin

CASTING	STAGE MANAGER	GENERAL PRESS AGENT	MUSICAL THEATER ASSOCIATE PRODUCER
Janet Foster	Thom Widmann	Philip Rinaldi	Ira Weitzman

GENERAL MANAGER	PRODUCTION MANAGER	DIRECTOR OF DEVELOPMENT	DIRECTOR OF MARKETING
Adam Siegel	Jeff Hamlin	Hattie K. Jutagir	

MUSIC DIRECTION

Ted Sperling

MUSICAL STAGING

Jonathan Butterell

DIRECTION

Bartlett Sher

OPENING NIGHT: APRIL 18, 2005

Front cover photo by Joan Marcus; Design by Evan Gaffney
Back cover photo of Adam Guettel © 2005 Anita & Steve Shevett
Production photos by Joan Marcus

ISBN 1-4234-0386-X

WILLIAMSON MUSIC®

A RODGERS AND HAMMERSTEIN COMPANY

www.williamsonmusic.com

EXCLUSIVELY DISTRIBUTED BY

HAL•LEONARD®
CORPORATION

7777 W. BLUEMOUND RD. P.O. BOX 13819 MILWAUKEE, WI 53213

Visit Hal Leonard Online at
www.halleonard.com

BIOGRAPHY

Adam Guettel is a composer/lyricist living in New York City. His newest musical, THE LIGHT IN THE PIAZZA (cast album on Nonesuch Records), with a book by Craig Lucas, premiered on Broadway at Lincoln Center Theater's Vivian Beaumont Theater in April 2005, following a world premiere at Seattle's Intiman Theater in Summer 2003, and a second engagement at Chicago's Goodman Theater in early 2004 (where it received three Joseph Jefferson Awards including Best Musical). THE LIGHT IN THE PIAZZA received 6 2005 Tony® Awards including two for Mr. Guettel—Best Original Score, and Best Orchestrations. PIAZZA also received 5 Drama Desk Awards, including two for Mr Guettel—Best Music, and Best Orchestrations. He wrote music and lyrics for FLOYD COLLINS (cast album on Nonesuch Records), which received the 1996 Lucille Lortel Award for Best Musical and earned Mr. Guettel the Obie Award for Best Music. FLOYD COLLINS has been presented at Playwrights Horizons, New York; Prince Theatre, Philadelphia; Goodman Theatre, Chicago; Old Globe, San Diego; Bridewell, London; and elsewhere. His other works include LOVE'S FIRE, a collaboration with John Guare for The Acting Company, and SATURN RETURNS, a concert at Joseph Papp Public Theater/New York Shakespeare Festival. SATURN RETURNS was recorded by Nonesuch Records under the title MYTHS AND HYMNS. Four of Mr. Guettel's songs were featured on Audra McDonald's Nonesuch Records album, WAY BACK TO PARADISE (1998), and two more appear on her 2000 album, HOW GLORY GOES (including the title track). Mr. Guettel himself performed a concert evening of his work at New York's Town Hall in 1999. Film scores include ARGUING THE WORLD, a feature documentary by Joe Dorman, and the score for JACK, a two-hour documentary for CBS by Peter Davis (1994). Accolades for Mr. Guettel include the Stephen Sondheim Award (1990), the ASCAP New Horizons Award (1997), and the American Composers Orchestra Award (2005).

When Adam Guettel was born in December, 1964, his grandfather, Richard Rodgers, and his mentor-to-be, Stephen Sondheim, were deep in preparation for the Broadway opening, just three months later, of what would be their only collaboration: the musical DO I HEAR A WALTZ? It was not a happy experience for either man, and the show was not a success. And yet you have to wonder what seeds were sown. Adapted from Arthur Laurents' 1952 play THE TIME OF THE CUCKOO, the musical told the story of an emotionally stalled American woman who, against all odds, opens herself up to the possibilities of love during a visit to Venice. Forty years later this same theme turns up, with variations, as the core of Guettel's new musical, THE LIGHT IN THE PIAZZA. Such is the ravishing power of this piece you almost feel that he was compelled to return to the time of his birth, to that unfulfilled collaboration of his artistic ancestors, so he could retrieve the reins of the classic American musical and get it back on track.

THE LIGHT IN THE PIAZZA is a wondrous fable that is as simple and complicated as its ineffable subject, love. Its setting is Italy, summer, 1953. A well-off, middle-aged woman from Winston-Salem, Margaret Johnson (Victoria Clark), has been dutifully dragging her twenty-something daughter, Clara (Kelli O'Hara), to all the sights, Baedeker in hand. In a square in Florence, a breeze separates Clara from her hat, which is promptly rescued by a handsome young man, Fabrizio (Matthew Morrison).

Clara has a secret that would seem to make romance an unlikely, perhaps even dangerous proposition. Fabrizio, who works in his father's tie shop by the Arno River, seems barely past boyhood and speaks little English. How this young couple overcomes these obstacles—and how Clara's mother is liberated from her own disappointments in love and life by her child's unexpected rapture—is the show's drama and the only drama it needs.

The musical's book, written with characteristic empathy and humor by the playwright Craig Lucas, has been adapted from a novella by the American writer Elizabeth Spencer that has never been out of print since it was first published in *The New Yorker* in 1960. (It was also made into a Hollywood film, starring Olivia de Havilland as the mother, in 1962.) Spencer's vision of Italy, in which invading Americans attempt to negotiate the Old World with fixed ideas and mixed results, overlaps with that of Henry James—but is remade by her astringent, no-nonsense Southern candor and by historical circumstance. PIAZZA unfolds in the midst of "the Italian miracle," when the Marshall plan and tourist dollars like the Johnsons' are lifting a society out of its fascist shadows and its defeat in the war. This is the Italy of Anita Ekberg and early Fellini and De Sica, of mythic American interlopers both real (Tennessee Williams) and imagined (Patricia Highsmith's talented Mr. Ripley). It's a culture in flux and a far cry from the naïve, rather self-satisfied 1950s America of the Johnsons' suburban upper-middle class. In the Lincoln Center Theater production, the staging by Bartlett Sher and production design by Michael Yeargan (sets), Catherine Zuber (costumes), and Christopher Akerlind (lighting), turn Italy, with all its voluptuous mysteries, both de Chirico–esque modern and ecclesiastical antique, into a major character in the show.

THE PIAZZA

BY FRANK RICH

In his previous works, Guettel has pursued a vein so specifically American that it's hard to picture him in Firenze. FLOYD COLLINS (1996), true to its real-life tale of a Kentucky man who was trapped in a cave in 1925, is saturated with Southern folk influences even as it for the first time sets out the distinctive dimensions of Guettel's own plaintive voice. The song cycle MYTHS AND HYMNS (1999) acknowledges the spare classicism of 19th century New England hymnals even as it draws on the musical vocabulary of contemporary American pop. There is no Americana in THE LIGHT IN THE PIAZZA. A few sweet bows to various Italian musical idioms notwithstanding, this is a score tied to no place or time; it aspires to leave behind such diurnal specifics and soar to the realm of pure emotion. In that, it echoes Clara and Fabrizio, who can only come together if they find a language of love that transcends all cultural, social, and linguistic barriers. As Fabrizio's father says of the couple in Spencer's novella, "They are in the time of life when each touch, each look, each sigh rises from the heart, the heart alone."

This is what Guettel captures in his music. It's indisputably Richard Rodgers territory, but if the feelings here can run as deep as those in the undying Rodgers love songs, the vulnerable romanticism in PIAZZA is unmistakably Guettel's own. Almost as if he were conducting an unconscious dialectic with NO STRINGS (1962), another late, post-Hammerstein Rodgers musical about Americans seeking love on the continent in the 1950s, the PIAZZA score is almost all strings. From the first ethereal bar of the overture there is a shimmer and reach to the melodies that breaks through the traditional boundaries of the Broadway number. It's as if Guettel were determined to capture the golden light of Tuscany in a bottle. The title song— sung by Clara in Act II, when Fabrizio and the possibility of happiness seem fatally out of reach—just keeps surging and surging into the heaven that so transfixed the Guettel of MYTHS AND HYMNS. In its dramatic placement, melodic beauty, and evocation of the sensation of sheer youthful yearning, there is not much in the American musical that can match it, unless it's the ballet by the fatherless daughter, Louise, danced in part to the strains of "If I Loved You" in Act II of CAROUSEL.

Such is the expressiveness of the music that the show's Italian passages require no translation to be understood. But Guettel's lyrics are remarkable as well. "Now is I am happiness," sings Fabrizio as he tries to muster any English he can to convey his joy to and for Clara. "Never I am unhappiness / Now is I am happiness with you." The song is called "Passeggiata," and it takes the form of a jaunty promenade as the young man proudly invites the American girl he loves at first sight to "walk with me in the place that I know." Rarely has inarticulateness been so articulate. "His innocence protects him like magic," wrote Spencer of Fabrizio—and it's just that direct, uncalculated pureness of spirit that emerges through the boy's broken syntax and makes us fall in love with him too. Yet it's essential to both Fabrizio's character and the character of the entire musical that at a certain point words disappear entirely, in this song and others, to be supplanted by gorgeous arias that are all music, as if lovers' hearts really were in their throats.

"Love! Love! Love if you can, oh my Clara," sings the girl's mother as the story reaches its moving denouement. "Love if you can and be loved." It says everything about the brilliance of THE LIGHT IN THE PIAZZA that this sentiment, not exactly a new one in the history of the musical theater, emerges here as a stunning revelation, in all its innocence and all its passion, as if no one had ever thought of singing about it before.

CONTENTS

THE LIGHT IN THE PIAZZA

MUSIC AND LYRICS BY ADAM GUETTEL

BOOK BY CRAIG LUCAS

"An ambitious new show that reaches for the sky!"

– New York Times

To learn more about THE LIGHT IN THE PIAZZA and the other great musicals
available for production through R&H Theatricals,
please visit our website
www.rnhtheatricals.com
or contact

229 W. 28TH ST., 11th FLOOR
NEW YORK, NEW YORK 10001

PHONE: (212)564-4000
FAX: (212)268-1245
E-MAIL: theatre@rnh.com

The offering of this publication for sale is not to be construed as authorization for the performance of any material contained herein.
Applications for the right to perform THE LIGHT IN THE PIAZZA, in whole or in part, should be addressed to R&H Theatricals.

The R&H Concert Library is Proud to Represent
SYMPHONIC SUITE FROM *THE LIGHT IN THE PIAZZA*
Music by Adam Guettel   Arranged by Jonathan Tunick

For information contact The R&H Concert Library at:
Tel: 212-268-9300 Fax: 212-268-1245 E-mail: concert@rnh.com

Statues and Stories

Words and Music by
Adam Guettel

Allegretto moderato

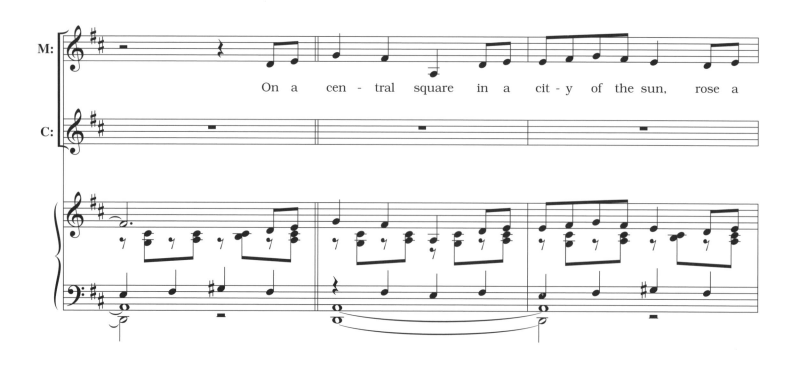

On a cen-tral square in a cit-y of the sun, rose a

Più mosso

Poco rit.

A tempo

The Beauty Is

Words and Music by
Adam Guettel

Agitato (*Moderately slow 4*)

CLARA:

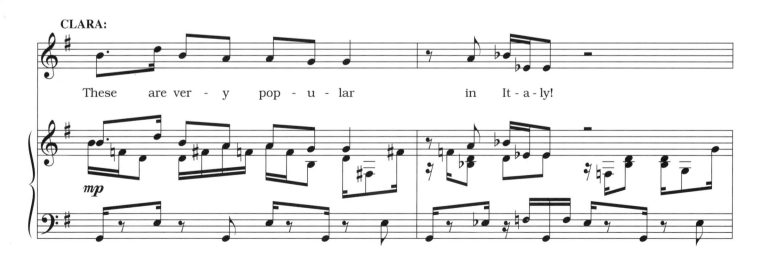

These are ver - y pop - u - lar in It - a - ly!

It's the land of na - ked mar - ble boys!__

Some-thing we don't see a lot in Win - ston Sa - lem.

That's the land of cor - du - roys!__

Poco più mosso

I'm just a some-one in an

espr.

sub. legato

old mu - se - um, far a - way from home as some - one can go,

and the beau - ty is I still meet peo - ple I know._____ Hel -

Expressively

lo. This is want-ing some-thing. This is reach-ing for it.

This is wish-ing that a mo-ment would ar-rive. This is tak-ing chanc-es.

This is al-most touch-ing. What the beau-ty is...

I don't un-der-stand a word they're say - ing. I'm as dif-f'rent here as

dif-f'rent can be, but the beau-ty is I still meet peo - ple like me.

Poco rall. **Tempo I°**

Ev - 'ry-one's a moth - er here

23

in It - a - ly.   Ev - 'ry - one's a fa - ther or

a son.___   I think if I had a child___

I would take such care of her.___   Then I would - n't

feel like one.___   I've

Il Mondo Era Vuoto

Words and Music by Adam Guettel
Italian Translation by Judith Blazer

Romantically

mai. Cla - ra, la

lu - ce nel - la piaz - za.

Cla - ra, mia lu - ce, mio cor!

Or - a che so - no sve - glio all - 'om - bra non vo tor -

sen - za che mi man - ca - va sei tu. La tua lu-ce m'in-

on - da.

Ma lei non puo a-mar-mi! Non co-si! Oh Cla-ra!

Non a-mer-a un ra-gaz - zi - no! Non puo a - ma-re'un ra-gaz-

zi - no! Di - o! Pa - pa!

Cla - ra! Cla - ra! Cla - ra, mia lu - ce, mio

cor! L'es - sen - za che mi man -

ca - va sei tu. Sei tu

Cla - ra! Cla - ra! Cla - ra, mia lu - ce, mio

cor! L'es - sen - za che mi man - ca - va sei tu.

Sei tu Cla - ra! Cla - ra!

Cla - ra, mia lu - ce, mio cor! So - lo nel

Passeggiata

Words and Music by
Adam Guettel

Dividing Day

Words and Music by
Adam Guettel

Moderato con moto

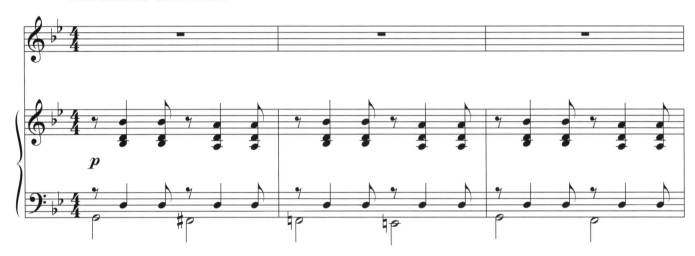

MARGARET:

Dash - ing as___ the day___ we met, on - ly

there is___ some - thing I don't re - cog-nize.___ Though I can - not name___

it yet,_____ I know it._____

Beau - ti - ful_____ is what_____ you are. On - ly some-how_____ wear-ing_____ a

frigh-ten-ing_____ dis - guise._____ I can see_____ the win - ter in_____ your eyes_____

_____ now,_____ tell-ing me:_____ "Thank you. We're

Does it go creep - ing slow - ly? When was your di - vid -

- ing day?

I can see___ the win - ter in___ your eyes___

___ now___ tell-ing me:___ "Mar - g'ret, we

did it. You curt - sied,___ I bowed.

Poco rall.

How could I__ have guessed? Was your cheek__ u- pon my chest,__ an

A tempo

o - cean__ a - way?_____ When was,

when was, when was di - vid - ing

day?_____

Say It Somehow

Words and Music by
Adam Guettel

The Light in the Piazza

Words and Music by
Adam Guettel

Con moto (*in 2*)

piaz - za. Ti - ny sweet,_____ and then it grows,_____ and

then it fills_____ the air.

Who knows what you call it. I don't care!_____

Accel.

Out of some-where I have some-thing

Tempo I°

I have nev - er had, and sad is

hap - py. That's all I see.

The light in the piaz - za.

The light in the piaz - za. It's

rush - ing up._____ It's pour - ing out._____ It's fly - ing through_____ the

air, all through the air. Who knows what you

call it. But it's there!_____ It is

Accel.

there!_____ All I see is,

Tempo Iº

all I want is tear - ing from in - side.

I   see   it!

Now   I   see

it   ev - 'ry - where!___   It's

ev - 'ry - where!_____ It's ev - 'ry - thing and

ev - 'ry-where!_____ Fa - bri - zi - o._____

The light in the piaz - za. My love.

Let's Walk

Words and Music by
Adam Guettel

Andante con moto

SIGNOR NACCARELLI:

I look at him and that was me,____ the blind-ness and the en-er-gy.____ I

want to say:____ "Here, come this way."____

MARGARET:

When we are at a cer-tain age____ we al-most fall on pur-pose, fall with

all our might,____ and then it is al-right. But what____

____ do I know____ of the road____ to be tak - en for

We might as well walk,_____ we might as well_____ walk..._____

walk...

Love to Me

Words and Music by
Adam Guettel

see._____ Oh_____

Oh_____

_____ You're not_____ a - lone!_____

Now I see as I have nev-er seen_____ be -

fore,_____ since that mo - ment in the

square_____ when your

hat is car - ried in the air_____

just so you can chase it,_____

just so I can be there. This is how I know.

This is what I see. This is love to

me.

Rit.

Fable

Words and Music by
Adam Guettel

Moderato ma non troppo

MARGARET:

You can look___ in the for - est   For a sec - ret field___

For a gold - en ar - - row

76

For a char - i - o - teer

For a fa - ble of love that will car - ry you

To a moon___ on a hill,___ to a hid - den stream___

_ A la-goon___ and a red___ ho - ri - zon dream___

legato

who looks___ for you.___

But   while you look___ you are chang-

-ing,   turn - ing   You're a well___ of wish -

es, you're a fal - len ap - ple.

Not the eyes,___ but the part___ you can't___ ex - plain

For the arms___ you could fall___ in - to___ for - ev -

- er___ For the joy___ that you thought___

You'd nev - er know___ For here___ at last___

mp

sub. p

cresc.

Rit.

That some - one knows_____ you

A tempo

Love!_____

Molto rit.

Love!_____

Poco meno mosso

Love_____ if you can,_____ Oh, my Cla - ra_____

Rall.

Rubato

Love_____ if you can_____ and be loved.

Più mosso

The Light in the Piazza

(PERFORMANCE EDITION)

Words and Music by
Adam Guettel

Con moto *(in 2)*

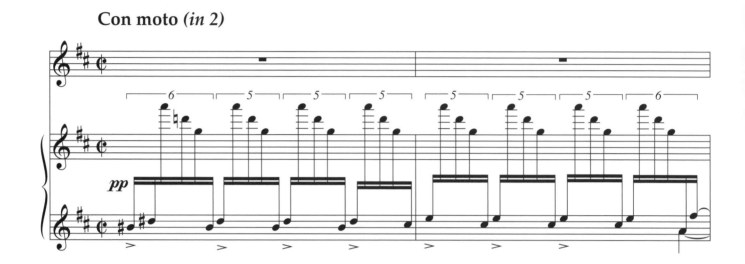

ev - 'ry - where! Fa - bri - zi - o.

The light in the

piaz - za. My love.

"ADAM GUETTEL, THE MOST GIFTED AND PROMISING THEATER COMPOSER OF HIS GENERATION, IS BACK, AND BETTER THAN EVER!"

— Wall Street Journal

ALSO AVAILABLE

Vocal Score
(HL00740127)

FLOYD COLLINS

MUSIC AND LYRICS BY Adam Guettel
BOOK BY Tina Landau
ADDITIONAL LYRICS BY Tina Landau

"This is *the* original and daring musical of our day
...a powerhouse."

– New York Magazine

Vocal Selections
(HL00313157)

MYTHS AND HYMNS: A Concert

MUSIC AND LYRICS BY by Adam Guettel

"Soaring...Guettel shoots for the moon
and arrives in style...A celestial journey"

– New York Newsday

AVAILABLE THROUGH **HAL LEONARD CORPORATION, EXCLUSIVE DISTRIBUTOR OF MATTHEW MUSIC AND WILLIAMSON MUSIC**

PERFORMANCE RIGHTS AVAILABLE THROUGH **R&H THEATRICALS**
www.rnhtheatricals.com

ORIGINAL CAST RECORDING ON **NONESUCH RECORDS**